MOLLY'S MAGIC CARPET

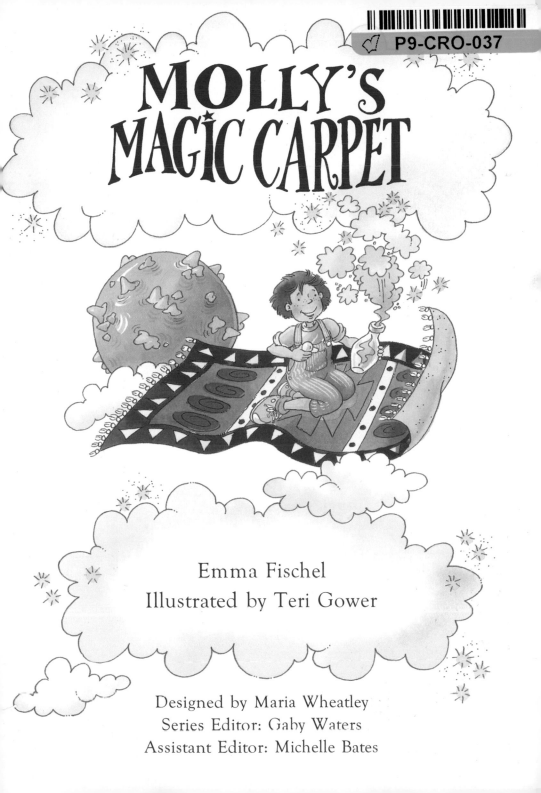

Emma Fischel

Illustrated by Teri Gower

Designed by Maria Wheatley
Series Editor: Gaby Waters
Assistant Editor: Michelle Bates

Contents

Meet Molly

This is Molly. She lives by the sea.

Today she is on her way to play. But there is an amazing adventure lying in wait for her. Just follow her outside to find out more.

Keep your eyes open for clues. If you get stuck, there are answers on pages 31 and 32.

Molly Takes a Tumble

"To the rescue!" shouted Molly, charging down the steps. Today she was a brave knight, off to tame a dragon.

CRASH!

BANG!

WALLOP!

She went tumbling and landed with a big, hard bump.

"Ouch," she said and rubbed her bottom. "That hurt."

"Well, look where you're going next time," grumbled a little voice.

Molly jumped. Who had said that?

4

"Get your muddy feet off my back. You'll get my pattern dirty. And tie your shoe laces."

Molly was baffled. She looked around her. There was no one outside. But something had spoken to her. Something must be magic.

What do you think it is?

Up, Up and Away!

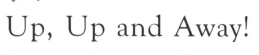

"You're a talking carpet!" Molly gasped nearly toppling over.

"A magic carpet," the voice corrected. "Well . . . almost."

It wriggled.

"The trouble is," it said, "I won't be a real magic carpet until I do something brave."

The carpet heaved a big sigh. "But I've been flying for days now and still can't find a single brave thing to do. And time's running out. Soon I'll become an *ordinary* carpet ~ no voice, no flying, nothing!"

The carpet curled up at one corner. "Maybe you could help me," it said.

"I~I'll try," said Molly. And before she knew it, the carpet lifted off the ground and they were up and away. Higher and higher they flew, up into the sky.

"Where are we going?" Molly shouted.
"Wonderworld!" cried the carpet. "We
head for the big blue moon, then fly
straight on until breakfast. Hold on tight."

**Here's Molly. Can you help her
find her way to the blue moon?**

Wonderworld

Wonderworld! What a sight it was!
On and on they flew, over gleaming
oceans and rolling hills, over magical
lands Molly had never even imagined.
They curved and swooped through the sky.
Molly felt light as a feather.

The wind rushed through her hair. The clouds flew by. Soon she felt as though she had been flying forever.

"I never want it to end!" she cried.

The carpet chuckled. "Cloudworld, Spookville, Topsy-turvydom, Monsterland, One Mountain Island, all below us," it sang out.

Which island do you think is which?

Rocky Ride

Just then, the carpet started to jiggle and jitter. Molly clung on for dear life.

"I'm running out of flying magic," the carpet gasped, spinning down toward the sea.

The wave tops came nearer and nearer . . . and so did a very large rock. Molly shut her eyes tight. THUD!

Molly opened her eyes. "We can hop from rock to rock to the beach," she said. "You might be able to," sniffed the carpet. "But not me. I'm far too tired. You'll just have to carry me."

Molly rolled the carpet up carefully, tucking it under her arm. Then someone shouted from the beach.

Safely Ashore

"Made it," gasped Molly, flopping down onto the sand.

"Unroll me, please," a muffled voice squeaked.

"Wow!" said the boy on the beach. "Can that thing really fly?"

"I am not a thing," said a small frosty voice. "I am a carpet. And a very special one at that."

"I beg your pardon," said the boy, eyes popping out of his head as the carpet spoke. "I'm Frank and this is my rabbit. Did you really fly here?"

"All the way," said Molly proudly. "Well almost."

"Can I have a turn?" Frank said eagerly.

"A turn?" the carpet snorted. "I'm not a fairground ride."

"We could fly to the Candy Café," said Frank.

The carpet liked the sound of that. So when it was rested, they set off.

"There it is," said Frank. "It's blue ~ next to the umbrellas."

Can you spot the Candy Café?

13

A Strange Sight

Bump! The carpet landed. Molly
gasped with astonishment. It
must be carnival day. There were
clowns and stilt walkers, jugglers
and acrobats.

Then . . . DONG! An
enormous gong boomed out.

What happened next was the strangest thing Molly had
ever seen. Everyone stopped moving . . . everyone except
Molly. They all froze to the spot like statues.

What was going on? Nobody spoke. Nobody moved.
Nobody did anything at all. Then . . . DONG! The gong
struck again.

All of a sudden, everyone sprang back into life . . . and into a little trouble.

Molly stood and gaped. "What happened?" she asked Frank. But he didn't answer. He was looking for his rabbit.

Can you see Frank's rabbit in this picture?

Magic Mix~up

"What happened just now is nothing new," sighed Frank. "It happens a lot and it's all the fault of Mort the magician."

Molly listened hard as Frank started to explain . . .

"Mort the magician lives in a castle at the very top of the mountain.

He used to do nice spells. But one day he sent an invitation and all that changed.

Watch me test my latest brilliant spell! Come to the blue lollipop tree at 2 o'clock sharp. Love from Mort

The whole town turned out to watch Mort do his magic.

The magic potion in this jar will turn vegetables into ice cream!

I open the jar, say the magic words . . .

Agga Zagga Doo Doo! And hey presto . . .

But the spell didn't quite do what it was supposed to. Little by little, Mort started to change before our eyes.

Everyone started roaring with laughter. Mort flew into a rage. He hated being laughed at."

I'll make you sorry you laughed at me. Just you wait and see!

Can you spot all the changes to Mort?

17

Molly Has a Plan

"So Mort thought up a brand new spell to pay us back for laughing at him," said Frank, leading the way to the Candy Café. "And now, any time he opens his spell jar, the blue clouds billow out and we all freeze to the spot. It's a dreadful nuisance."

"Can't you stop him somehow?" asked Molly.

"Only by taking the jar with the blue clouds in it," said Frank. "But it's hidden somewhere in his castle. We've tried flying up there . . . but there is nowhere to land. We've tried climbing . . . but he's covered the top in sticky toffee. We've tried everything we can think of . . . nothing works."

Candy Café - Ices, jellies and lots lots more

Molly thought hard as Frank finished his story. "There must be a way up," she said. "If the magician does it."

"But he uses magic," said Frank sadly.

"Then so must we," said Molly. "A magic carpet!"

Quick as a flash, the carpet shot off and hid. It didn't like the sound of Molly's idea at all.

Where is the carpet hiding?

Flying High

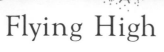

"This is your big chance, carpet,"
said Molly, hugging it. "Now
you can do something brave!"

"Well, I don't *feel*
brave," it said in a
wobbly voice. "But I
do want to be a
real magic carpet. So,
let's go!"

"To the top of the
mountain!" shouted Molly.

Soon the waving figures on the ground were just tiny
specks below them. Molly and the carpet were alone in
the big blue sky.

Up and up they flew. Past rivers that plunged into
foaming white falls. Past forests of dark, densest green.

The side of the mountain grew steeper and steeper.
The clouds rushed past. It grew colder and colder.

And all the while the castle grew closer and closer.

At last the huge castle loomed above them. Three magic birds circled around it, uttering strange harsh cries. Molly listened hard. They seemed to be trying to help her.

Can you spot the way into the dungeon?

Underground

The dungeon was stinky and dark. Slimy things dripped down the walls.

"Which way do we go?" Molly gulped. The carpet just shook like a leaf.

Then Molly saw a map. "This will help us," she said.

Can you find the way in?

Way into Castle.

WARNING! WATCH OUT FOR FIERY DRAGONS
AND SLITHERING SNAKES!

Dungeon
Entrance

You are
here
x

Surprises in Store

"We have to find the spell jar," gasped Molly. Then they whizzed around the castle so fast, it seemed almost as if they were in three places at once.

They tried big doors and small doors . . .

. . . stiff doors

. . . and creaky doors.

Until there was only one place left to look ~ in the highest tower of all.

But there was a shock in store at the top.
Not one magician . . . not two . . . but three!

"Surprise!" they all chortled. "Only one of us is real. But which one? Guess wrong and ~ PLOP! ~ in you go to my pot of stinky slime!"

Then the three magicians started to sing.

The one in stripes of red and blue
Will plop you in the slimy goo
The one in spots of green on blue
Is not the magic man for you
The one with yellow stars you see
Is he you want, you see he's me

**Can you spot the real Mort?
(The song will help you.)**

The Spell Jar

PFFF! Two of the magicians vanished in a puff of smoke. Molly and the carpet shot through the door and bolted it.

"You won that time," shouted Mort. "But bolts won't stop me and if I get to the spell jar first, I shall freeze everyone to the spot until Christmas!"

"Quick, look for a jar with blue clouds in it," said Molly.

Can you find the spell jar?

Homeward Bound

"Found it!" shrieked Molly. "Let's go!" Leaping onto the carpet, they soared out of the window.

Molly flung the spell jar up in the air. It hung for a moment then down it fell, faster and faster.

SMASH! It hit a rock and splintered into tiny pieces. A puffy blue cloud floated off into the sky.

"Spoilsports!" wailed a faint voice. "I'll never be able to make that spell again. It's gone forever!"

"And a good thing too," shouted Molly.

"Homeward bound," cried the carpet. "Hold on tight. It's a long way down!"

They played hide-and-seek with birds in the clouds.

They raced with shooting stars.

They surfed on the breezes.

They chased waterfalls down the mountainside.

Down and down they flew. And then Molly saw something she recognized. A tree she had noticed before that told her they were near their journey's end.

Which tree does Molly recognize?

Goodbye

"Made it!" gasped the carpet, landing smoothly.

"You brave thing," said Molly, squeezing it. She felt something.

"What's this?" she said. "A label?" She read it carefully . . .

"You've done it!" she said, hugging the carpet tightly. You're a real magic carpet now!"

"Imagine that!" it said, twisting to look at its shiny new label. "I suppose I must be!" And it curled up at one corner with pleasure.

"Then, waving goodbye to Frank and all their new friends, Molly and the carpet set off home. "I wish it didn't have to end," Molly sighed, snuggling down.

"This is only the start," smiled the carpet. "Who knows where we'll go next time!"

Genuine Magic Carpet

Answers

Pages 4-5

The magic thing outside is the carpet. Here it is, right under Molly's feet.

Pages 6-7

The way to the blue moon is marked here in black.

Pages 8-9

Did you know which island was which? You can see them here.

Monsterland

Topsy-turvydom

Cloudworld

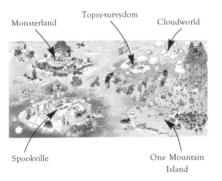

Spookville

One Mountain Island

Pages 10-11

The safe way to the beach is marked in black. This is the only way that avoids all the crabs and slimy squids.

Pages 12-13

The Candy Café is here.

Pages 14-15

Frank's rabbit is all tangled up under the carpet. Here he is.

Pages 16-17
All of the changes to Mort are circled here.

Pages 18-19
The carpet is hiding above the sign for the Candy Café.

Pages 20-21
The Ifflediffle plant hides the entrance to the secret passage. It is circled below.

Pages 22-23
The way into the castle is marked in black.

Pages 24-25
The real Mort is the one with yellow stars on his magician's coat. He is in the middle.

Pages 26-27
Here is the spell jar.

Pages 28-29
Molly recognizes the blue lollipop tree. She knows it means she is nearly back at the town.

This edition first published in 2002 by Usborne Publishing Ltd., Usborne House, 83-85 Saffron Hill, London EC1N 8RT, England. www.usborne.com Copyright © 2002, 1995 Usborne Publishing Ltd. The name Usborne and the devices 🔔 🔔 are Trade Marks of Usborne Publishing Ltd. All rights reserved.